S0-AAC-512

# Individual
## Preparedness and
## Response to
### Chemical, Radiological, Nuclear, and Biological Terrorist Attacks

# A Quick Guide

Lynn E. Davis, Tom LaTourrette
David E. Mosher, Lois M. Davis, David R. Howell

Supported by the
**Alfred P. Sloan Foundation**

**RAND**
**Public Safety and Justice**

The research described in this report was sponsored by the Alfred P. Sloan Foundation under Grant No. 2002-10-2. This research was conducted within RAND's Public Safety and Justice program.

ISBN: 0-8330-3487-1

RAND is a nonprofit institution that helps improve policy and decisionmaking through research and analysis. RAND® is a registered trademark. RAND's publications do not necessarily reflect the opinions or policies of its research sponsors.

*Cover design by Stephen Bloodsworth*

© Copyright 2003 RAND

All rights reserved. No part of this book may be reproduced in any form by any electronic or mechanical means (including photocopying, recording, or information storage and retrieval) without permission in writing from RAND.

Published 2003 by RAND
1700 Main Street, P.O. Box 2138, Santa Monica, CA 90407-2138
1200 South Hayes Street, Arlington, VA 22202-5050
201 North Craig Street, Suite 202, Pittsburgh, PA 15213
RAND URL: http://www.rand.org/
To order RAND documents or to obtain additional information, contact Distribution Services: Telephone: (310) 451-7002; Fax: (310) 451-6915; Email: order@rand.org

# PREFACE

This Quick Guide presents a strategy that individuals can adopt to prepare for and respond to terrorist attacks involving chemical, radiological, nuclear, and biological weapons. The strategy is designed to provide simple and clear guidance for individuals to help protect themselves in the event of an actual terrorist attack, which may involve extremely hazardous and unfamiliar conditions. Steps that individuals are now taking or might take to avoid such attacks are not part of this strategy.

These recommendations emerged from a study that RAND conducted, under the sponsorship of the Alfred P. Sloan Foundation, and is fully reported in *Individual Preparedness and Response to Chemical, Radiological, Nuclear, and Biological Terrorist Attacks*, Santa Monica, Calif.: RAND, MR-1731-SF, 2003.

This study was conducted within RAND's Public Safety and Justice program. RAND Public Safety and Justice conducts research and analysis that helps inform policymakers and communities in the areas of public safety, including law enforcement, terrorism preparedness, immigration, emergency response and management, and natural disasters; criminal justice, including sentencing and corrections policy, firearms, and community violence; and drug policy, which focuses on problems related to illegal drugs and substance abuse.

Inquiries about RAND Public Safety and Justice may be directed to

Jack Riley
RAND Public Safety and Justice
1700 Main Street
Santa Monica, CA 90407-2138
310-393-0411

# CONTENTS

# Acknowledgments

Many people have participated in this project and contributed in a variety of ways. We would especially like to thank our many RAND colleagues. Lisa Meredith and Terri Tanielian superbly led our focus group discussions; James T. Quinlivan, John Parachini, and Greg Jones helped us develop the terrorist scenarios; Charles Meade gave us a thoughtful review; and Paul Steinberg helped us conceptualize our effort. Very special thanks go to Phyllis M. Gilmore, who took up the challenge of translating our analytical report into this readily understandable Quick Guide. Thanks also go to Stephen G. Bloodsworth, whose many talents can be seen in our cover design and the enclosed reference card, and to Phillip Wirtz, who carefully proofread the results. Finally, this report benefited enormously from the support, counsel, and encouragement of K. Jack Riley, who leads RAND's Public Safety and Justice unit.

# INTRODUCTION

There is much the nation must do—and is doing—to guard against and prepare for terrorist attacks. In some possible situations, individuals may have to rely on themselves to protect their own health and safety—perhaps even their own lives. Thus, individual preparedness is an important element of our nation's strategy for homeland security.

Many people know how to respond in such disasters as fires and earthquakes, but few would know what to do if someone were to use a chemical, radiological, nuclear, or biological weapon in their vicinity. Although the characteristics of such attacks may vary widely and their likelihood is highly uncertain, they can all create unfamiliar and very dangerous circumstances. Consequently, individuals need an overall strategy they can use to prepare for and respond to such attacks.

This guide emerged from a detailed what-if, scenario-driven analysis we conducted to examine four types of terrorist attacks: chemical, radiological, nuclear, and biological.[1] In each case, the response strategy is guided by a fundamental objective, which we refer to as an *overarching goal*, which in turn depends on taking certain actions. We have distilled our findings into this guide to offer individuals a series of actions they can take to save lives, even in catastrophic situations.

The actions we present here are appropriate regardless of the likelihood of an attack, its scale, or

---

[1]A related RAND report—*Individual Preparedness and Response to Chemical, Radiological, Nuclear, and Biological Terrorist Attacs* , Santa Monica, Calif.: RAND, MR-1731-SF, 2003 (ISBN 0-8330-3473-1)—describes the supporting analysis and presents our strategy in greater detail.

the current government alert level; they are designed to be useful over a range of variations in scenarios; and they have been defined in terms of simple rules that should be easy to follow. The reference card included at the back of the guide encapsulates the key points and can be removed for display in a prominent place.

Note that any preparedness strategy will need to be refined and updated continually, as new opportunities for individual preparedness and response emerge, and to account for the evolving nature of the terrorist threat.[2]

---

[2]The Department of Homeland Security has taken an important step in launching the Ready campaign. A description of the various activities in this campaign can be found on its Web page: www.ready.gov. We view our recommendations as further developing these and other recent terrorism preparedness guidelines.

# Recommended Response Strategy: Chemical Attack

## Overarching Goal

*Find clean air very quickly.*

## Specific Actions

1. *If attack is outdoors, and you are outdoors, take shelter quickly in the closest building, close all windows/doors, and shut off the flow of air. If inside, stay inside. Then, to the extent possible, move upstairs, find an interior room, and seal the room. Remain inside until told it is safe to leave, and then ventilate and vacate the shelter immediately.*
2. *If attack is indoors, follow chemical attack plans specific to your building. If these are not available, open windows and breathe fresh air. If open windows are not accessible, evacuate (using escape hood if available) by stairs to street or roof.*
3. *Once protected from chemical agent exposure, decontaminate by removing clothes and showering.*
4. *When conditions are safe to move about freely, seek medical treatment.*

Chemical attacks entail the dispersal of chemical vapors, aerosols, liquids, or solids, and individuals are affected by inhaling these or being exposed

through their eyes and skin. Terrorists could use any of numerous chemical agents in an attack, including both industrial chemicals and chemical warfare agents. Chemical weapons act very quickly, often within a few seconds. As a result, government officials are unlikely to be able to give warning or guidance. Individuals must act almost instantly and on their own to minimize exposure.

It is critical to know whether the attack has occurred outdoors or inside a building and to take action according to where you are in relation to that release. It is essential to find clean air very quickly.

If the chemical attack is outdoors, and you are outdoors, take shelter inside and close all doors and windows. If possible, also shut off the airflows. This provides protection by keeping out the chemical agent. However, because buildings cannot be sealed off entirely, you need to vacate the building as soon as it is safe. Knowing when it is safe will likely require guidance from emergency officials. Evacuation in such attacks is not recommended because individuals cannot determine soon enough where it would be safe to evacuate to. Neither is using respiratory protective equipment recommended in an outdoor chemical attack because it would only be effective if put on within a minute or less, and this is probably not feasible.

Finding clean air is particularly challenging in an indoor chemical attack, given the variations in ventilation systems. Consequently, it is best to follow a chemical attack response plan designed specifically for the particular building. This is not always possible, particularly in unfamiliar buildings. If you do not know the specific plan for the building, the fastest way to find clean air is to open a window or door to the outside. If that is not possible, either because the window or door will not open or none is available, evacuate the building using the stairs, going either to the street or, if it is closer and known to be accessible, to the roof. Because there is a risk that you might need to move through areas with dangerous concentrations of chemical agents, using an emergency escape hood can make evacuation safer.[3] However, because escape hoods are expensive and require advance training, using one may not be an option for many individuals. You should evacuate the premises whether you have a hood or not because the alternative of sheltering in an interior space creates potentially more serious dangers.

Once you have obtained a reliable source of clean air, your next concern is the residual danger chemical agents may present. It is thus important to begin personal decontamination as soon as possible. This means removing and bagging your clothing and washing yourself thoroughly with soap and water.[4]

Finally, given the range of possible medical effects of chemical agents, anyone potentially exposed should also seek medical care.

---

[3]An emergency escape hood is a soft-sided pullover hood with an elastic neck seal. These hoods provide chemical and biological air filtration for 15 to 60 minutes, enabling the wearer to exit dangerous environments. Because there is no face seal, these hoods do not need to be fitted to the individual and are compatible with eyeglasses and facial hair. Users need proper training in the use of hoods (as well as with any other respiratory protection). Escape hoods should only be used when they have been issued as part of a workplace or other organizational safety program.

[4]Emergency officials will inform you about how you should treat or dispose of contaminated clothing.

# Recommended Response Strategy: Radiological Attack

## Overarching Goal

*Avoid inhaling dust that could be radioactive.*

## Specific Actions

1. *If an explosion occurs outdoors or you are informed of an outside release of radiation and you are outside, cover nose and mouth and seek indoor shelter. If you are inside an undamaged building, stay there. Close windows and doors and shut down ventilation systems. Exit shelter when told it is safe.*
2. *If an explosion occurs inside your building or you are informed of a release of radiation, cover nose and mouth and go outside immediately.*
3. *Decontaminate by removing clothing and showering.*
4. *Relocate outside the contaminated zone, only if instructed to do so by public officials.*

A radiological attack is likely to entail use of what is often called a "dirty bomb," in which conventional explosives are used to disperse radioactive material quickly across a wide area. Beyond the risk of immediate injury from the explosion itself, the primary initial danger is inhaling the radioactive material that is suspended within the dust and smoke from the explosion. A secondary hazard is the danger that residual radiation presents for those who remain in the contaminated area for a very long time. In either case, the levels of radiation will be quite low, so the main concern is an elevated risk of cancer, which will only manifest itself after many years.

The authorities are unlikely to detect the radiation immediately, so you will need to be able to respond on your own, without knowing whether or not radiation is present. Your primary goal is to avoid inhaling dust that might be radioactive. Note that, even though the fact that the dust is radioactive will not be clear at first, many other types of dust also present serious health hazards and should likewise be avoided. So, it is advisable to take the actions we describe here in case of any explosion.

For an outdoor explosion, if you are outside, take shelter inside the nearest undamaged building; if you are inside an undamaged and unthreatened building, stay there. If the explosion occurs inside your building, get out. You can further protect yourself by covering your nose and mouth. A dust mask (one with an N95-rated particulate filter) would be most helpful, but any cloth available will do, such as a shirt.

Immediate evacuation of the area is not recommended, for two reasons. First, you could not evacuate quickly enough to avoid inhaling potentially radiation-laden dust. Second, you are unlikely to know where to go to be safe or even how to get there safely, since you will have little way of knowing the direction the contaminated dust is moving and where it is settling.

After safely finding shelter, anyone who might have been exposed to the radioactive material should begin to decontaminate themselves immediately. As with chemical exposure, this means removing and bagging your clothing, then washing yourself thoroughly with soap and water. You should also seek medical attention after officials indicate that it is safe to do so.

Although contamination levels from a radiological weapon are likely to be quite low, the concern about the effects of long-term exposure may be great enough in some areas that authorities will ask you to leave your home or business for an extended period.

# RECOMMENDED RESPONSE STRATEGY: NUCLEAR ATTACK

## Overarching Goal

*Avoid radioactive fallout: evacuate the fallout zone quickly or, if not possible, seek best available shelter.*

## Specific Actions

1. *Move out of the path of the radioactive fallout cloud as quickly as possible (less than 10 minutes when in immediate blast zone) and then find medical care immediately.*

2. *If it is not possible to move out of the path of the radioactive fallout cloud, take shelter as far underground as possible or if underground shelter is not available, seek shelter in the upper floors of a multistory building.*

3. *Find ways to cover skin, nose, and mouth, if it does not impede either evacuating the area or taking shelter.*

4. *Decontaminate as soon as possible, once protected from the fallout.*

5. *If outside the radioactive fallout area, still take shelter to avoid any residual radiation.*

A nuclear detonation will be unmistakable the moment it occurs: It will be marked by blast effects strong enough to knock over buildings, a brilliant flash of light, high-energy radiation, and extreme heat. The explosion will produce a characteristic mushroom cloud, from which radioactive material will begin to fall after about 10 to 15 minutes. The area affected by this fallout will be long (extending tens of miles downwind) and narrow (spreading only a few miles). Given the potential destruction and disruption caused by such an attack, it may take several days for officials to be able to offer guidance or support.

Warning about a terrorist nuclear attack is unlikely; hence, there is little chance of protecting yourself from the immediate blast and radiation effects. However, even after these immediate effects, a tremendous hazard will remain from the radioactive fallout. This fallout is highly lethal. It is thus critical for your survival to avoid the fallout, either by evacuating the fallout zone quickly or by seeking the best available shelter.

Evacuation—getting completely out of the path of the radioactive cloud—is a highly effective way to protect against fallout. But time matters because you will have less than 10 minutes when in the immediate blast zone. Because the distance you will need to travel will be relatively short, at most a mile or so, you will be able to do this by foot. The key to evacuating quickly is to find the right way out. This requires effort but is not as difficult as it may seem at first. The cloud will cover a portion of the blast zone, so anyone there should move directly away from the blast center (away from the location of the initial bright flash and from the greatest damage) until clear. The approximate location of the rest of the radioactive cloud can be determined by observing the direction in which the wind is blowing the cloud. You should move perpendicular to the wind direction until you are out from underneath the cloud. Once you are out of the fallout zone, you should find medical care immediately.

If evacuation is not possible, you must find appropriate shelter immediately. Sheltering from nuclear fallout requires getting as much solid material (dirt, concrete, or masonry) and space as possible between yourself and the radioactive fallout. The best shelter is deep underground. If you cannot get to an underground shelter before the radioactive fallout begins to arrive, the next-best shelter would be on the upper floors of a multistory building (greater than ten stories), at least three stories below the roof to avoid the fallout deposited there. You must stay inside this shelter for at least 24 to 48 hours to allow the radioactivity of the fallout to decline to safe levels.

Keeping your skin, nose, and mouth covered as you move out of the path of the radioactive cloud can provide some additional protection, but do this only if it causes no more than a few moments delay in evacuating the fallout zone or finding shelter. Once you have protected yourself from the fallout, you should decontaminate yourself as described earlier.

Even those who are located outside the fallout zone should take shelter, preferably in the basement of a house or building, given the uncertainties about exactly where the radioactive cloud will travel.

## Recommended Response Strategy: Biological Attack

### Overarching Goal

*Get medical aid and minimize further exposure to agents.*

### Specific Actions

1. *If symptomatic, immediately go to medical provider specified by public health officials for medical treatment.*
2. *If informed by public health officials of being potentially exposed, follow their guidance.*
   - *For contagious diseases, expect to receive medical evaluation, surveillance, or quarantine.*
     - *If "in contact" with persons symptomatic with smallpox, obtain vaccination immediately.*
   - *For noncontagious diseases, expect to receive medical evaluation.*
     - *For anthrax, obtain appropriate antibiotics quickly.*
3. *For all others, monitor for symptoms and, for contagious diseases, minimize contact with others.*
4. *Leave anthrax-affected area once on antibiotics if advised to do so by public health officials.*

Biological attacks can involve either contagious or noncontagious agents. Some agents (possibly anthrax) can survive in the environment for a very long time and cause further risk of exposure if they become resuspended in the air.

Unlike the other scenarios we have discussed, it may take days for a biological attack to be recognized and for the specific agent to be identified. The diseases biological agents cause each have their own timelines; identification usually comes after the incubation period for the disease, which, in some cases, may be two weeks or more.[5]

This means the government will play a central role in identifying the attack and guiding individuals about what to do. At the same time, the government will face many challenges in providing appropriate medical care, especially when many essential services may be disrupted. You will thus need to be ready to act on your own, even when the government is providing guidance, to get medical aid and minimize further exposure to the agent.

It will be critical for you to find out whether or not the biological agent is contagious and whether or not you have been exposed. With that information in hand, you should then be prepared to follow the specific instructions for the particular agent involved. Below, we discuss the specific guidance that individ-

---

[5]Note that this discussion also applies to other biological agents besides organisms and viruses. Some examples are the botulinum toxin (which causes botulism) and ricin. Although the effects of these agents are essentially chemical, the consequences of the attack might not be realized for hours or even a few days. Thus, the appropriate steps to take would be similar to those for an attack involving noncontagious biological agents.

uals could expect to receive today for smallpox (which is contagious) and anthrax (which is not contagious).

Once the attack and the agent have been identified through clinical diagnosis, public health officials will provide information about the symptoms and instruct you to get medical treatment immediately if you display any of them. Anthrax can be prevented or cured with aggressive use of antibiotics. Although smallpox has no cure, medical care increases the chances of survival.

You might have been exposed to the agent if you were in the vicinity of the attack or, in the case of a contagious agent, have been exposed to someone who was there or who has subsequently contracted the disease. In these cases, there is a heightened probability that you may have been infected but are not yet showing symptoms. Public health officials will work to identify such individuals.

For contagious diseases, you should expect and closely follow guidance from public health officials not only about symptoms but also about the possible need for a medical evaluation, medical surveillance, or quarantine. In the case of smallpox, you can become infected by being in the release area within two days of the time of the attack or by being in contact with someone who has already been infected with smallpox. Because smallpox is thought to be contagious from the time a patient develops a rash until scabs have formed (a period of approximately 12 days, beginning 12 to 16 days after infection[6]), it

---

[6]D. A. Henderson et al., "Smallpox as a Biological Weapon: Medical and Public Health Management," *Journal of the American Medical Association*, Vol. 281, 1999, pp. 2127–2137.

is critical that individuals who have close contact with such persons obtain a smallpox vaccination as quickly as possible.[7] Smallpox is the only known potential biological weapon for which vaccination after exposure has proven value, if given within three to seven days of the exposure. If, however, it takes more than seven days to identify a smallpox attack, officials are unlikely to recommend vaccination for those who had been in the area at the time of the attack because it will be too late for vaccination to be effective.

For noncontagious diseases, you should expect and closely follow guidance from public health officials not only about symptoms but also about the possible need for a medical evaluation and, in the case of anthrax, the need to receive antibiotics, a critical defense against the development of anthrax. You have the potential for being exposed to anthrax if you have been in the release area at any time since the attack.

There is considerable uncertainty about how likely it is for anthrax spores released in the air to become airborne again once they have settled on the ground. As a precaution, officials may recommend or require that people in the infected area relocate to avoid long-term dangers.

---

[7]According to the Centers for Disease Control and Prevention, those at risk are individuals who have come into close contact with an infected person while that person is contagious, as well as household members of those who have come into close contact. *Close contact* means living in the same home as someone who has smallpox or spending at least three hours in the same room with someone who has smallpox. (Centers for Disease Control and Prevention, *CDC Smallpox Response Plan and Guidelines*, Draft 3.0, 2002, online at http://www.bt.cdc.gov/agent/smallpox/response-plan/index.asp [as of August 22, 2003].)

Because biological attacks will most likely not be detected until many days later, the threat of being infected by the release is long past by the time individuals become aware of an attack. Thus, there is no practical benefit at that point to taking shelter or wearing dust masks with particulate filters. To be useful, protective measures would need to be in place at the time of exposure. So, we discuss these below as a useful preparatory action. If an attack were, however, identified at the time, use of such a mask and finding shelter would provide effective protection.

# RECOMMENDED RESPONSE STRATEGY: PERSONAL PRIORITIES

> 1. Act first to ensure your own survival.
> 2. Take steps to decontaminate yourself.
> 3. Help others if it is safe to do so.
> 4. Make contact with family/friends.

In the midst of an unfamiliar and dangerous situation, whether a natural disaster or a terrorist attack, it is tempting to act according to certain human instincts. It seems perfectly natural to stop to help others or to try to contact family and friends. But, especially in the situations we are discussing here, taking the time to do so could well put your own survival at risk and might hinder that of others. Having a clear set of overall priorities is essential so that you can and will take the recommended actions quickly.

Your first priority is to survive. Then, given the dangers that radiological dust, radioactive fallout, and chemical agents present to the human body, you must decontaminate yourself. Recognize that you may not be able to help anyone else; most individuals are not qualified to provide the kinds of medical treatment that would be needed in cases of the attacks described here. Finally, you should not attempt to contact family or friends until you have ensured your own safety.

# What You Can Do to Prepare Yourself

> 1. Gain understanding of what will be required to accomplish response actions in each type of terrorist attack; learn to recognize attack characteristics; understand the response actions.
> 2. Facilitate response actions by making plans and gathering information in advance: develop family communications plan; plan for long-term shelter; learn about appropriate kinds of medical treatment from medical professionals; discover building evacuation plans and potential shelters.
> 3. Ensure general emergency kit accounts for terrorist attacks: dust mask, battery-powered radio, duct tape and plastic sheeting.
> 4. Enhance protection through passive steps: weatherize home, install good-quality particulate filters.

Preparing yourself in advance will help you accomplish what you need to do in all these types of attacks. The most important preparation is gaining an understanding of what you must do and why. Beyond this, you can make specific plans for yourself and your family. These plans should include making a communication plan and providing for long-term shelter. It will also be useful to learn about what kinds of medical treatment will be appropriate and to discover building evacuation plans and potential shelters.

It is also important to have a personal emergency kit for terrorist attacks. This kit should include a few essential items: One is a dust mask with an N95-rated particulate filter, which will protect against radiological dust and fallout, as well as biological agents. These are inexpensive, readily available, and easy to store at home, at work, and in the car. Another is a battery-operated radio, which could be a critical tool for receiving information about when it is safe to vacate shelters and other instructions from government officials after chemical, radiological, and nuclear attacks. In the event of a chemical release, duct tape and plastic sheeting would be useful for sealing openings that could admit chemical agents into your shelter.

Finally, you can improve your protection against an undetected biological attack by implementing permanent measures to help keep biological agents out. One way to do this is to create a barrier, for example, by weatherizing your home. Another way is to install high-quality particulate filters on heating and ventilation systems, which can help remove contaminants from indoor air.

## What Government and Business Can Do

1. Inform individuals about official terrorism response plans.
2. Design education and training programs to explain and practice response actions.
3. Implement terrorist attack detection and warning systems.
4. Regulate and provide usage guidelines for retail equipment marketed for terrorism response.

Governments and businesses can also take important steps to help individuals learn and carry out appropriate responses to terrorist attacks. The actions these groups take will be important to everyone's ability to understand and carry out an appropriate response strategy.

The more that individuals know about government plans for emergency and other kinds of medical treatment (vaccinations and antibiotics), decontamination steps, possible relocation plans, and how such information will be conveyed, the better prepared they will be to respond appropriately and the more likely they will be to comply with what officials suggest. Beyond simply providing basic information, governments and private industry can spearhead formal education and training programs, to take knowledge from theory to practice.

Moreover, the introduction of detection and warning systems could improve the ability of individuals to survive different terrorist attacks—perhaps significantly.

Finally, it would be useful for government and businesses alike to ensure that products marketed for terrorism preparedness and response are safe and effective. This would include setting standards for equipment design and performance, developing guidelines for product use, and supplying warning labels.